W9-AYU-221

LEARN TO DRAW...
FLOWER GARDEN!

Written and designed by Heather Zschock

Illustrated by Kerren Barbas Steckler

PETER PAUPER PRESS, INC.
White Plains, New York

For Emily, Audrey, and Jake

PETER PAUPER PRESS

In 1928, at the age of twenty-two, Peter Beilenson began printing books on a small press in the basement of his parents' home in Larchmont, New York. Peter—and later, his wife, Edna—sought to create fine books that sold at "prices even a pauper could afford."

Today, still family owned and operated, Peter Pauper Press continues to honor our founders' legacy of quality, value, and fun for big kids and small kids alike.

Illustrations copyright © 2015 Kerren Barbas Steckler

Designed by Heather Zschock

Copyright © 2015
Peter Pauper Press, Inc.
Manufactured for Peter Pauper Press, Inc.
202 Mamaroneck Avenue
White Plains, NY 10601
All rights reserved
ISBN 978-1-4413-0557-2
Printed in China

Published in the United Kingdom and Europe by
Peter Pauper Press, Inc., c/o White Pebble International
Unit 2, Plot 11 Terminus Road
Chichester, West Sussex PO19 8TX, UK

7 6 5 4 3

Visit us at www.peterpauper.com

Hey, young artists!

Are you ready to learn how to draw 47 different flowers, birds, and more? It's easy and fun! Just follow these steps:

First, pick a tulip, butterfly, or other picture you want to draw. (You might want to start with the daisy . . . it's pretty simple.)

Next, trace over the picture with a pencil. This will give you a feel for how to draw the lines.

Then, following the numbered boxes, start drawing each new step (shown in red) of the picture in the empty space in each scene, or on a piece of paper.

Lastly, if you're an awesome artist (and of course, you are!), try drawing a whole scene with one or more of the flowers, insects, or things you would find in a garden. And remember, don't worry if your drawings look different from the ones in this book—no two flower gardens are exactly alike!

You are well on your way to creating beautiful garden masterpieces!

GET READY! GET SET! DRAW!

Daisy

1.
2.
3.
4.

Carnation

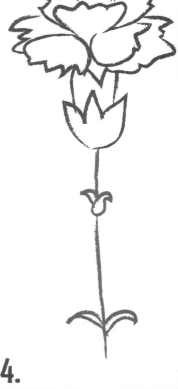

1.
2.
3.
4.

Bee

1.

2.

3.

4.

5.

6.

Beehive

1.

2.

3.

Rose

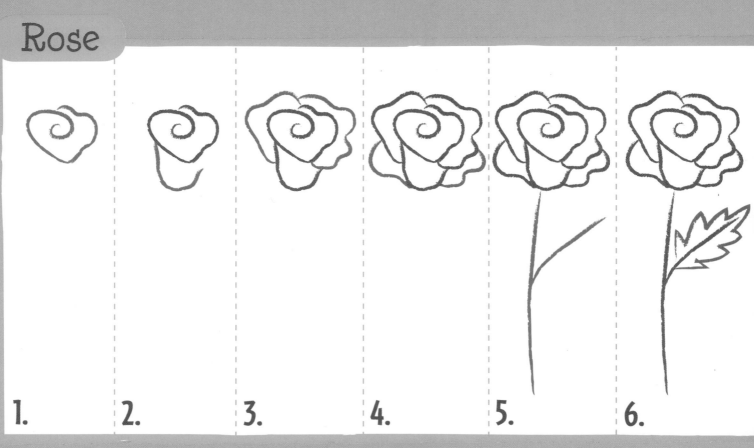

1.

2.

3.

4.

5.

6.

Bouquet

1.

2.

3.

4.

5.

6.

Bird

1.

2.

3.

4.

5.

Birdbath

1.

2.

3.

Iris

1.

2.

3.

4.

Allium

1.

2.

3.

4.

Trace over me for practice!

Butterfly

1.

2.

3.

4.

5.

6.

Hummingbird

1.

2.

3.

4.

5.

6.

Morning glory

1.

2.

3.

4.

5.

6.

Honeysuckle

1.

2.

3.

4.

5.

6.

Birdhouse

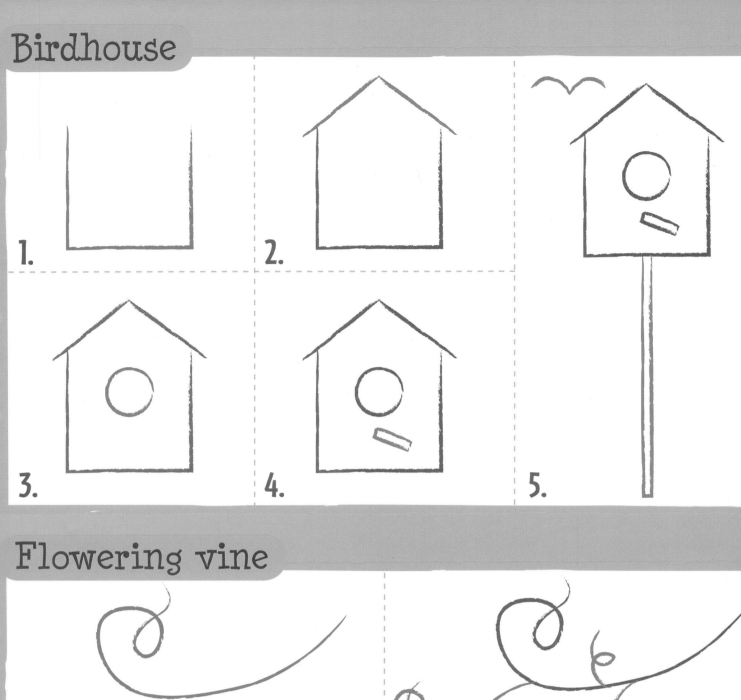

1.
2.
3.
4.
5.

Flowering vine

1.
2.
3.
4.

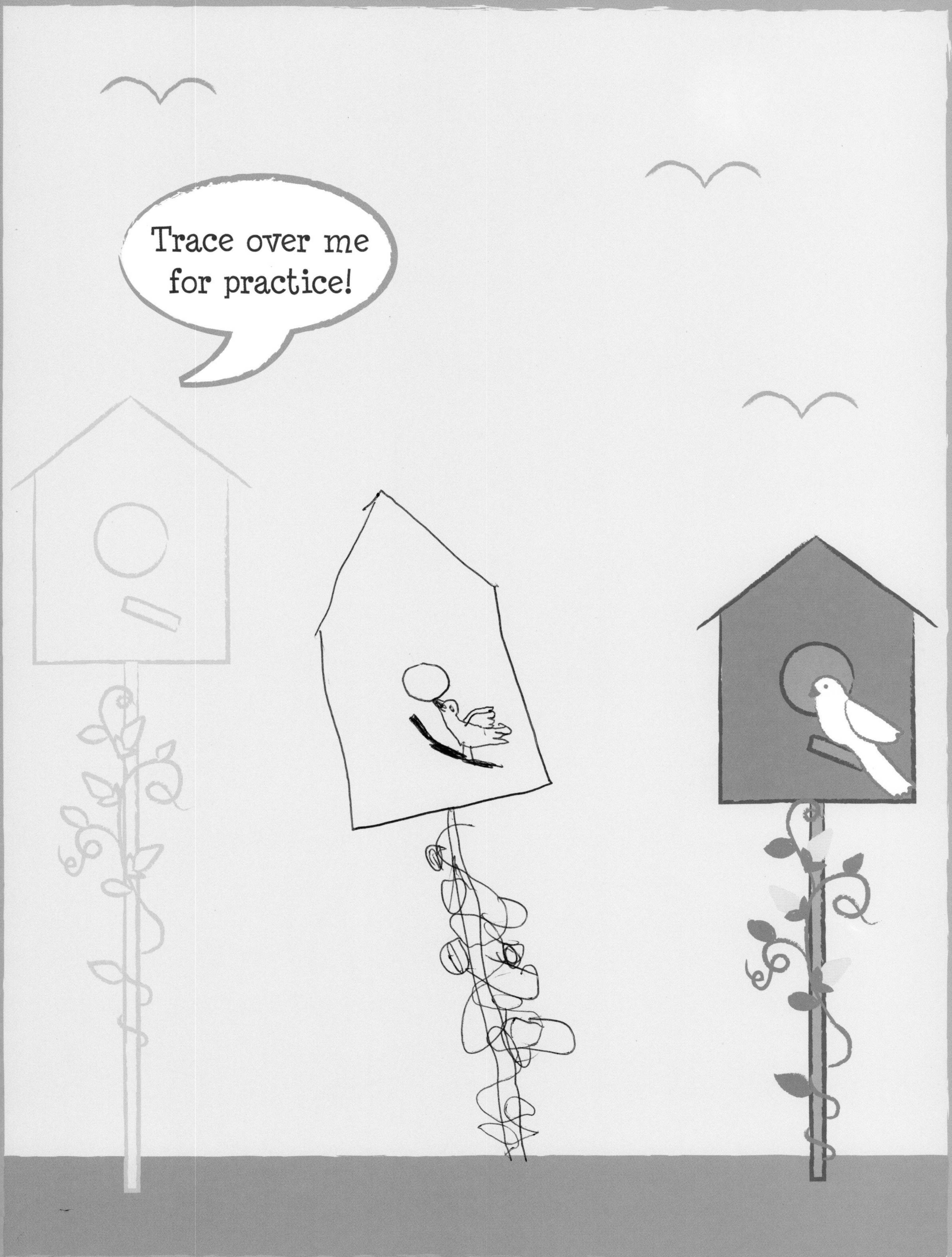
Trace over me
for practice!

Pansy

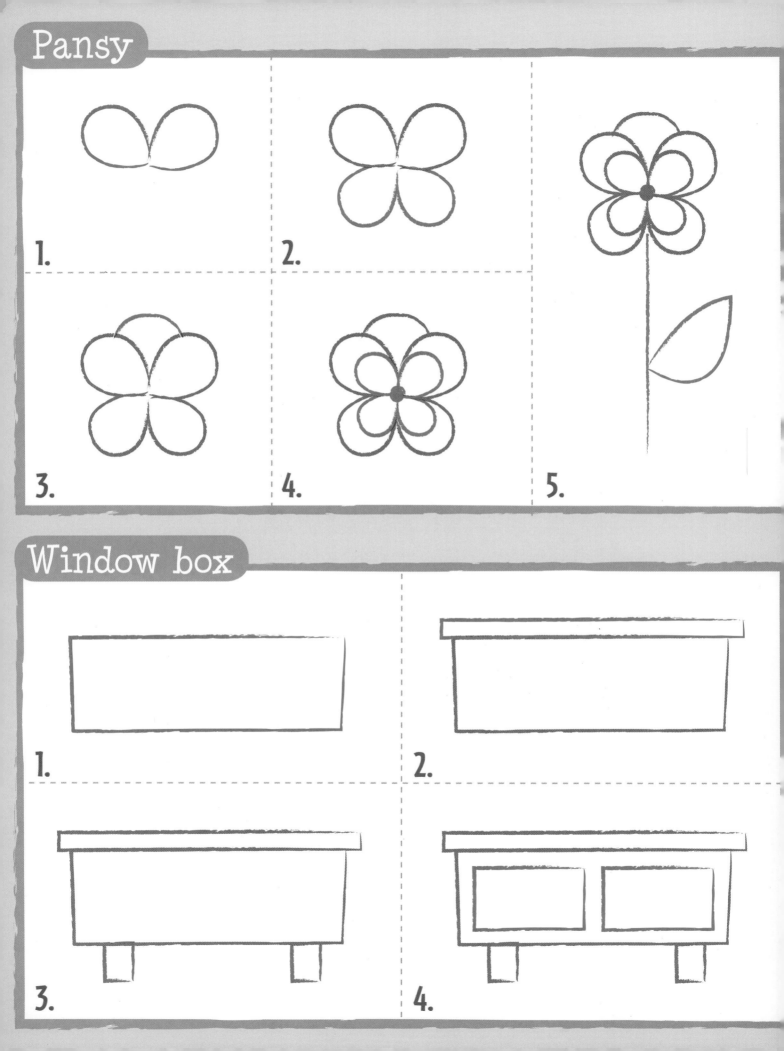

1.

2.

3.

4.

5.

Window box

1.

2.

3.

4.

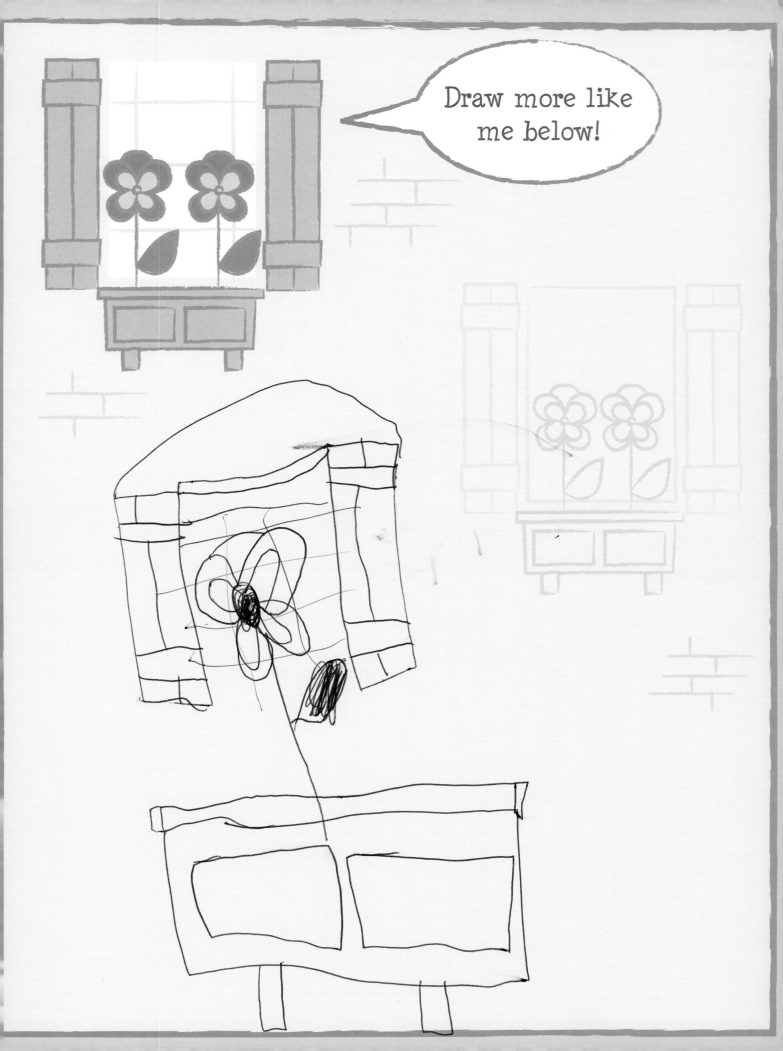

Ladybug

1.

2.

3.

4.

5.

6.

Worm

1.

2.

3.

4.

Poppy

1.

2.

3.

4.

Poppy buds

1.

2.

3.

Cloud

1.

2.

3.

Watering can

1.

2.

3.

4.

5.

6.

Seedlings

1.

2.

3.

4.

Sunflower

1.

2.

3.

4.

5.

Picket fence

1.

2.

3.

4.

Geranium

1.

2.

3.

4.

Trowel

1.

2.

3.

Flowerpot

1.

2.

3.

Trace over me for practice!

Tiger lily

1.

2.

3.

4.

5.

Vase

1.

2.

3.

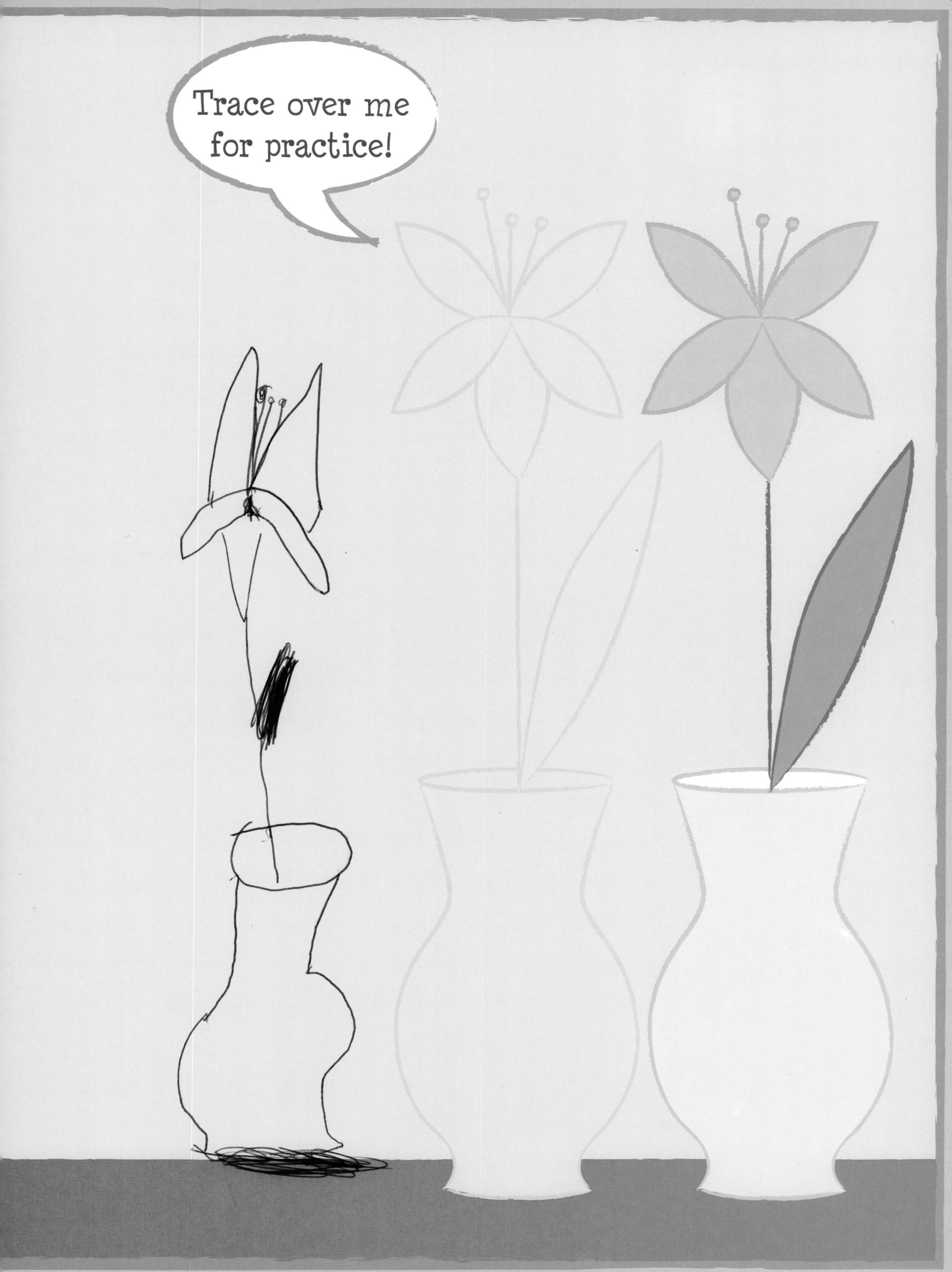
Trace over me for practice!

Wheelbarrow

1.

2.

3.

4.

Rake

1.

2.

3.

Garden tool

1.

2.

3.

4.

5.

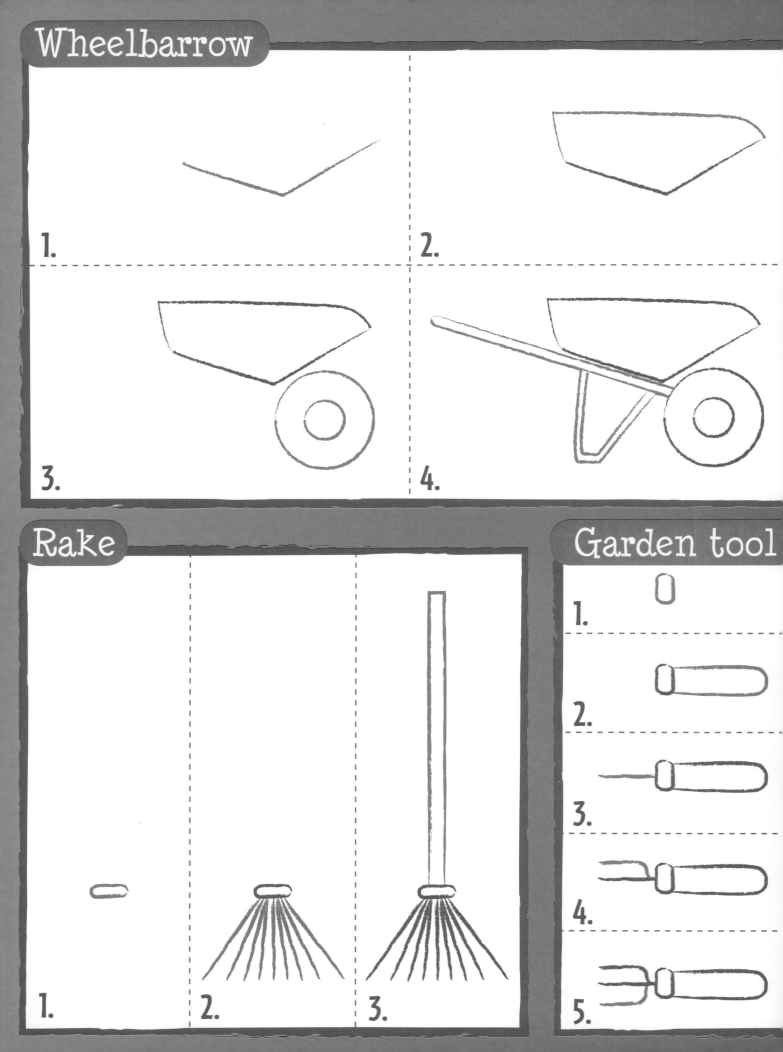

Daffodil

1.

2.

3.

4.

5.

Tulip

1.

2.

3.

4.

Trace over me
for practice!

Water lily

1.

2.

3.

4.

5.

6.

Frog

1.

2.

3.

4.

Peony

1.

2.

3.

4.

5.

Hydrangea

1.

2.

3.

4.

5.

Draw more like me above

Cherry blossoms

1.

2.

3.

4.

Cherries

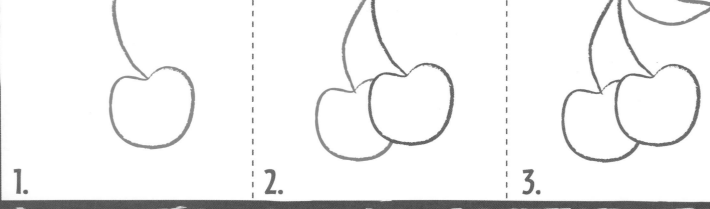

1.

2.

3.

Lupine

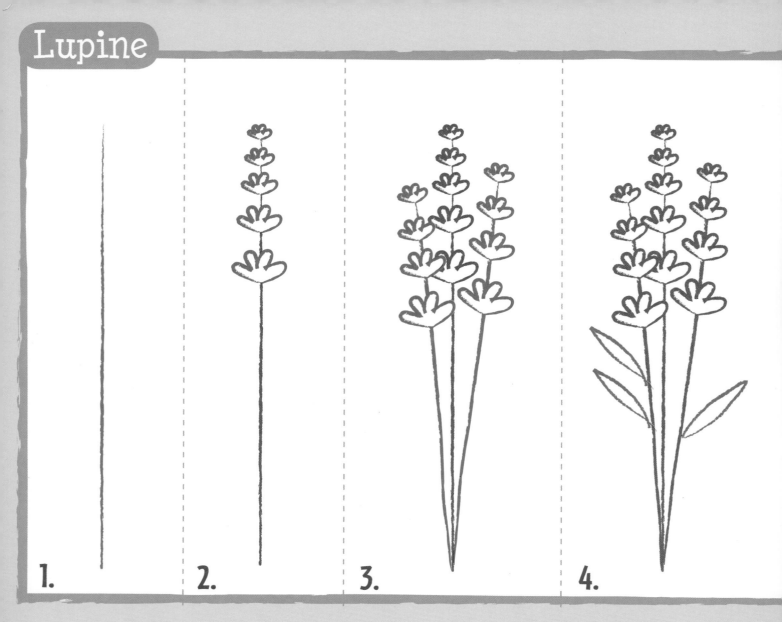

1. 2. 3. 4.

Lily of the valley

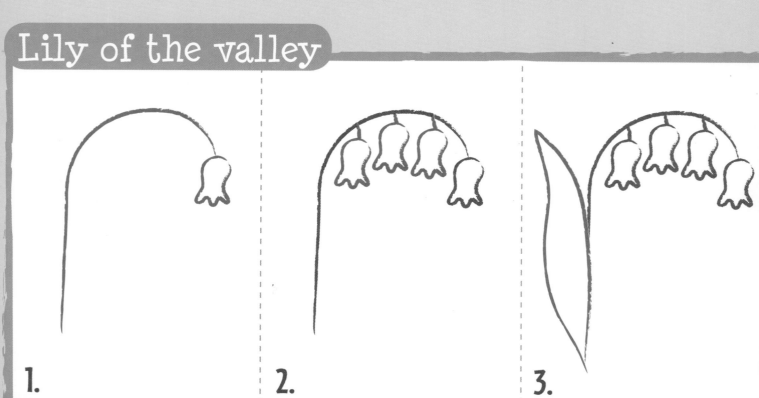

1. 2. 3.

Strawberries

1.

2.

3.

4.

5.

6.

Blossoms

1.

2.

3.

4.

Trace over me for practice!

Plant some ideas,
and what will grow soon,
is a garden of flowers
to blossom and bloom!